In the Wake of Dying

Lynne Nesbit

Published by Beccles Books Ltd
1 Exchange House, Exchange Square
Beccles, Suffolk NR34 9HH

The right of Lynne Nesbit to be identified as the author of this work has been asserted by her in accordance with Section 77 of the Copyright, Designs and Patent Act 1988.

ISBN 9781728869735

First Edition

First published in 2018

DEDICATION

I dedicate this book of poems to my Masters of Meditation,
whose unerring wisdom and guidance has removed from my
mind the fear of death.

Although, in all honesty, I cannot ignore a slight whiff of
trepidation at the thought of some disorientation, followed
by general dilapidation, certain deterioration and possible
disintegration before my own final dematerialisation, I have
not even the slightest whiff of doubt that my beloved
Teachers will be there, as they are now, to support me
through everything when the time comes. We shall cross
that bridge whenever... together.

My gratitude knows no bounds

Lynne Nesbit

Contents

IN THE WAKE OF DYING

PERHAPS

Perhaps death isn't the closing of a door,
the stemming of a flow.
Perhaps it's the opening of a floodgate,
the ability to know.

Perhaps death isn't the silent culmination of a noise,
the final bar-lines in the ear.
Perhaps it's the symphonic rhapsody of joy,
the ability to hear.

Perhaps death isn't cause for mourning
the loss of a life.
Perhaps it's the freedom from all fears,
the absence of strife.

Perhaps death isn't the end of all our being,
the pulling of the rug.
Perhaps it's another great beginning -
a divine, ecstatic hug

of welcome

to a life beyond our dreams,
where nothing merely "seems",
where everything is light and we its beams.

ETERNITY

It seems like a very long time to wait
once I've gone through that pearly gate

Yet I've sussed it out – the name of the game -
forget that there's anything ever the same

Except it is - of course - ever the same
in the place where I'll no longer have a name

I've wrestled, tussled with the phenomenon
of passing time when the moment's gone

It's impossible for the mind to see
how there is nothing but Eternity

We sit in our bubble and bounce along
believing we know the words of the song

but the music has neither beginning nor end
Just a few bar-lines between which we spend

a minim or two - or a semi-breve
if we're given a dream life with some reprieve

But I have the feeling we'll get the last laugh
It will all become clear at the end of the path

I'll turn up at the gate
thinking I'm late

and then float away in a room without walls
on a bed of roses where no petal falls

ON LIFE AND DEFT

How deftly we die
That very last moment is effortless
Out of the confines of the body -
we can leave that to the confines of the coffin
 Free at last!
Yet the approach, yes, the approach was such hard work
struggling to come to terms with a life's struggles
determined to terminate
perhaps forced to finish the job, because that's the nature of
death
That's what gives death life
But it's also death's sting – the sting in the tale-end
And we move forward
Bounce back off frayed ropes
to enter another affray
the umpteenth round
What shall we play next time?
Haply a different tune

ON MOVING ON

When I die, it'll be such fun –
All those jobs I've not begun
will wait forever, still undone.

I'll sit on a cloud with my Rooibosch Tea.
I won't be wondering whom I'll see
or whether they remember me.

My body, resting in its grave,
will moulder. There's nothing left to save.
None will notice how I behave.

I've been corked up for far too long.
I shall be singing a different song
as my bottle shatters when God sounds the gong.

!!Alleluja!!

BATHROOM STATIONERY

Yes, my life is a story
written on the flimsiest of tissue
easily torn, disintegrating
in a light shower of misfortune –
a wrong step taken,
someone else's carelessness,
or cellular malfunction of the worst kind.

My epitaph, however,
will stand the test of time
carved in stone.
How ironic!
But maybe not so...
a record, perhaps, of deeds, of qualities.

That's what remains:
memories of deeds and qualities.
My thoughts and feelings
are flushed down the pan.
But my deeds...
my qualities...
Watch what you do!
Watch how you do it!
It might be carved in stone...

...Until a generation's gap
eclipses the light of memory
and even those carved letters
will erode, vanish,
as flimsy as my bog-roll life.

DEATH AND TRANSFORMATION
Reflections in Dentdale

I am realising, with reluctance,
that to transform myself, I must die.
Every day, I must watch something of myself die.
My own body is the perfect symbol of transformation:
cells die and are reborn,
yet I remain like the horizon
which marks the line of the dale,
while grass, stones, streams, trees, sheep and people
come and go beneath it.
I look for symbols.
Read the signs.
Hear the messages.
I gather them all into my arms and bring them
into my heart's remembrance.
Every day I live a little...every day I die a little.
Like this valley.

MOONCLOUD

No moon tonight.
Clouded; cloud-hid;
Deep, dark summer-cloud shrouded.

Looking for a moonbeam;
Just a hint, a glint of moongleam
To show me that the clouds aren't real.

I want to feel that those clouds aren't real,
Merely wisps and wraiths,
Like passing faiths in this or that.

A NEW RELATIONSHIP

You came into her life by stealth.
Somehow, through the back door,
you slipped in and waylaid her.
She was unaware,
laid the way bare for you
and you entered, penetrated
deep into the marrow of her being,
a canker in the heart of her rose.

Though canker you were
and canker you remain,
she welcomed you all the same,
unafraid, "grateful for the privilege", she said,
though you led her a merry dance.
Would steal her wealth.
But once spied,
she denied you nothing.

She left nothing to chance.
Life took on a new perspective.
With respect, she engaged.
Though uninvited, you've been accepted.
She feels no dis-ease, no desire to please.
Indeed, to please would be fatal.
You're on equal terms now.
Stable.

WAITING FOR THE DOCTOR

They sat together,
he pensive, eyes downcast,
she, holding his hand,
glancing sideways
to catch his look;
both waiting
for the moment of truth.

"Do come in. Sorry I'm late."
They both rose.

THE PATIENT

She walked, face to the wind,
towards the hospital gates.
Dark skin, ash grey,
clung to her cheekbones,
taut around her jaw.
Her clothes flapped loose
over her spiky body.
Her eyes, haunted by some spectre
beckoning her to a destination
where white coats prevail,
held no light.
She held between her fingers
the only light in her life,
which cast its own shadow,
and her silvery lips drew long draughts from it.
We passed each other
and my heart met hers
(though she knew it not)
as she walked into the wind.

HOSPICE

Hospice – a soft sound which will seep
through every crack in your disbelieving chest
as it rises in hope
and falls in resignation from the very top of your being
and you can no longer hold that pose
which life forced on you at such cost.

Outside, a feathered host chirrups its springtime song
but that's not the post to which your mind's cortege can
hitch.
No, now the inner music thunders
and, spiced with new savours,
gives these last moments
an unfamiliar flavour of hospice.

AN OPEN DOOR

Forty-six years old –
He would be forty-six years old.

If she hadn't seen him lying there,
if she hadn't been a witness to his death,
the moment of moments
in his life and hers,
would he be here still?

The silence in his room
trickled out from beneath the door,
stealthy, all-pervading,
from beneath his bedclothes,
now unmoved and unmoving.
God moves, though, and His ways are mysterious.

Birthing into unquestioned simplicity
her baby had no expectation from life.
Expectation was not in his vocabulary.
He lived from perfect moment to perfect moment.

She had opened the door onto the ultimate Happening.
And now she could see.... through an open door....
how silence loses its stealth;
how light dispels darkness.
And now she can honour the wishes of the dead –
that is - to die.

GRIEF

The night at home
All alone
No-one can phone
I'm a stranded whale on a lonely beach

There is no light
There's no delight
I can't even fight
And you are so beyond my reach

All joy is gone
Can't see the sun
I feel quite numb
But grief attaches like a leach

Grief, grief, grief
A stealthy thief
Comes to find
My peace of mind
And steals it

REQUIEM

She listened, remembering grief
She saw a woman weeping, weeping
She listened, remembering the relief
She felt the music seeping, seeping
into her very marrow,
into parts made narrow

She listened, remembering her life
She listened and saw through tears still new
She saw a woman facing strife on strife
She saw how she, the woman, grew,
Each time a new path taken,
another world awakened

FAREWELL TO JIM

Sun streaming
Music wafting
Flowers perfuming
Coffin waiting...

Mourners gathering
Memories storing
Tears weeping
Coffin waiting...

Pews gleaming
Carvings flowing
Gold leaf shining
Coffin waiting...

Stories telling
Songs consoling
Light shafting
Coffin waiting...

Minds inspiring
Hearts uplifting
Joy arising
Coffin shouldered...

Arriving!

SHAFTED

We were shafted,
shafted by lanced beams of light.
But some would say
he was shafted,
shafted by God.
He had so much more to do,
they would say.
They wouldn't know,
they couldn't know
what he now knew.

IT'S A PROCESS....

"I'm not at my best," she said.
"Then let it rest," I replied.
"I've only just arrived. I've been away," she said.
My friend had been far away.

Marooned in sadness;
A lagoon of tears for her to cross.
To arrive on the journey called 'mourning'
is to reach a mere staging post.

We are mourners all our lives.
We may open new windows for virtually anything:
Click on "new"; start afresh.
Yet our mourning hasn't ended.

It vanishes, suspended somewhere on life's screen,
overlaid by virtual living.
"I've only just arrived," she said. But where?
"I'm not at my best," she said. For whom?

My friend's light still shines bright.
It illumines each window.
Her worst is others' best.
Her best is to die for.

And for the rest, we shall mourn together,
opening windows onto a bright morning.

WHEN

When can I say goodbye?
When can I even try
To thank you?

When can I hold your hand?
What about the things we planned
Together?

When can I sympathise?
Look directly in your eyes,
Say I love you?

LONG DARK NIGHT

The gnawing sadness, the disbelief
this is what I feel as grief
Lying awake in the long dark night
wondering if they're alright

I know we're feeling all the same
I know we share the aching pain
I know this is communal grief
I know it's a common disbelief

But knowing doesn't help at all
My reasoning begins to pall
I take my pen, begin to write
dry-eyed weeping
the long dark night

THE PITY OF IT

Ululating Yemeni women
Forgotten, not on my atlas, not here
Crying their unceasing grief
Pitted roads, pitted lives
No olives to pit
The unguent of tears, not oil,
is all they have
to pour into gaping wounds
and gaping doorways
Not here, not on my atlas, forgotten

DEREK – A NON SEQUITUR

The thin veil –
Life and death in the balance.
Translucent skin taut over parched white lips.
Milky-eyed, sunken deep into memories past.
Pupils misting into an ebbing tide.
Derek listened to his visitor.
He rose. "Would you like a plastic bag?"

WHITE ELEPHANT

The old man's phone rang and rang and rang.
He knew it was his. But what to do?
He pulled it slowly out of his pocket, turned it over and over,
Like a shell he had just found on the beach,
Or a piece of nostalgia on a white elephant stall.
It stopped ringing. Ah!
He put it to his ear then, but which way?
He couldn't hear anything at all, nothing from either end.
No matter – at least it had stopped ringing....

VACANT WITHOUT POSSESSION

Gone to lunch!
No-one is home.
The windows are open.
Anyone could walk through the gaping door.
But what would they find?
An empty mind.
Visitors are floored.
A brain which used to know at first cock's crow
the day's business,
a brain occupied with busy business,
clickety clack along its tracks.
"Here I am for you, and you, and you."
But rarely for her, it seemed.
She who lived and loved and cooked and cared for him.
But it was rare he was there for her.
He only opened certain rooms of his house
while she tiptoed like a mouse
around his requirements.
And now he's hardly ever there.
No-one at home.
She is alone,
still caring,
not daring to live her own life.
She keeps clean her own slate,
not to tempt fate.

AFTER THE FUNERAL, DENT CHURCHYARD

She came back after they had gone,
bending over the grave, picking at the flowers.
The ground was raw like an open wound.
Those blooms laid over to soothe and cover
glowed stark and gaudy in the clear light.
She read the messages one by one.
A small figure in a space
flanked by the village on the one side
and the impassive dale on the other,
stretching between one world's end and another.
She leaned against the graveyard's stone wall,
looked out from today's new boundary.
The pattern of the dale remained unchanged
yet her life, and his, spun in the vortex of reformation.
Movement in stillness, spiral passing through eternity,
through the grave.

THE WIDOW

Widow, widow, longing, looking
over the cemetery wall.

Clothed in black, feeling lack
in a life beginning to pall.

He's over there. His soul is bare
and ready to hear her call.

She longs to join him, lie beside him
and once more feel the thrall.

They will embrace and, together, face
some great and loving ALL.

THE QUICK AND THE DEAD

How could he compete?
To meet at right-angles
leaves no chance
to dance with death.
The quick fox could not jump this time.
The lazy cat was supreme.
And we, too, sped over his entrails
newly pink, wetly exposed, harshly drawn
in a picture of life so roughly torn.
Who would think that the other side of the road,
in the life of a fox,
could bode death?

Lynne Nesbit

LAND OF HOPE AND GLORY

Such a great sorrow wells up within me
I listen to Elgar's Coronation Ode
I am grateful to be English in England
The music is great
My feelings are great
Yet both leave my heart aching
That, at a time of peace declared and war over,
In the hearts of men war never ended

Eight million heroic horses died
Thousands sold to French and Belgian butchers
Betrayal! Iniquitous betrayal!
And we continue to butcher each other
My heart aches for all our lost men, women and children
All our lost homes
All our lost values,
My word is no longer my bond...

All those dead and still dead
And more, and more and more
The world is becoming one open grave
First World War, Second World War, Third, Fourth, Fifth
Knives drawn
Cutting deep into Humanity's Heart
Bleeding us to more death, ever death
My heart aches, sorrow wells up and brims over.

W A R!

The word, the very letters –

W-A-R!

The spike of bayonet
The deep-dug trench
Jagged splinters, shards of **W**
W oh W!
Your brave peaks
Your bestial valleys

W-A-R!

An endless cry of pain
From the first wince
Through the long-sighed **AHHH**
Breathing its last with rose-red **R**
R trembles with fear
Rumbling the stomachs of the fleeing
R growls with anger
Rumbling the guns which paint a bloody sky

W-A-R!

Once begun, once uttered
There is no closure....

WHAT MATTER DEATH?

What will it be like when I die?
Will I fly up to some place in the sky?
Will I be looking down from on high?
Or is there nothing?

Will I have time to say goodbye?
Will everyone heave a long, deep sigh?
Will anyone even bother to cry?
Or will there be no-one?

I'm beginning to think, as I heave my own sigh,
That none of this will ever apply,
That it's really a matter for you and I
To trust in the process, accepting no lie
And to live life now with the joyful cry:

There is no thing BUT LOVE!

ON LOSING A FATHER

How careless I was!
I must have lost you somewhere en route,
but I don't know where.
One moment you were there
and the next moment –
you weren't.

I've started to look for you now.
I've had some success.
Keep turning up little pieces of you
like shards of a broken pot.
Others have often got there first
but they are willing to share shards.
The archaeology of my father.
Your history dug up,
seen through many eyes.

Your pot is larger than I thought.
Larger than life.
As I find the pieces,
I find more than I thought I lost.

IT'S FINE TO DIE

When Dad died it was all okay because
Henry asked him how it was.
"I'm fine", he said, with a great big grin,
And I knew St Peter would let him in.
And when it's my turn to make that leap
I know it won't be eternal sleep.
A bit of a roller-coaster, I've no doubt,
Through the dark and finally out
Into a light that never ends,
Into a space which is peopled with friends.

THROUGH THE VEIL

I was tangled in the web of my dreams.
Suddenly, the web dissolved;
the dream's story suspended;
and there you were -
distant, small, waving somewhat diffidently
unsure, it seemed, whether I could see you;
you had slipped into my dream –
always the opportunist waiting for the right
moment.

"Can she see me through the veil?"
Dad, I saw you through the veil,
distant, small, waving as you always did,
standing in the road
or hanging out of your window until I was out of
sight.

Today, the veil, its filaments like grey silken gauze,
grew fine enough for a momentary glimpse.
And then I remembered Mum.
Instantly she appeared standing by your side
and I saw you both arm in arm,
smiling.

IN MEMORIAM - A WEEK LATER

The remaining bouquets,
Limp and lifeless,
Were tied still to the roadside railings.
Love tokens
To the late twin, the lover, the son,
The one who no longer resides
In his limp and lifeless body,
The body which couldn't rail
Against a moving metal machine.

Last week, new flowers freshly tied,
Remembering a young life
Cut off in its prime,
The pain of loss oozing from their stems.
A week later?
Well, the sap of a token
Doesn't keep rising forever.
It dries up.
Nature's emblems wither and fade.

But the sap of love,
Love's lifeblood,
Rises forever in the heart's memory.
A week, a year, a lifetime
Passes through the windswept heart
Without blowing away one atom
Of the twin, the lover, the son,
The one forever fresh, no longer tied,
Never late.

KIRKYARD, SCONE

Cool and green under the trees,
little mossy mound
marked by a little mossy headstone.
Cherubim forever watch over the spot
where Alice's corpse lies.
"Alice, aged thirteen months.
So beloved"
The stonemason made poetry out of the stone.
Tiny babe and tiny cherubim together,
cherished by Nature over the centuries.

Lynne Nesbit

FOR MOURNERS OF A CHILD

The band of those that mourn their dead
  increases, increases.
They stride the centuries with hearts
  in pieces, in pieces.
I gaze into my neighbour's eyes
  still spouting, oh, spouting
with tears of grief and puzzlement
  and doubting, yes, doubting
if life can offer recompense
  for losses, more losses
to every soul that had to bear
  such crosses, great crosses.
Yet every soul which seeks a birth
  is coming and going.
Deep in the heart of everyone
  is knowing, wise knowing.
Has known it long till it's replaced
  by yearning, deep yearning.
And God finds those who have no need
  for learning, more learning.
He plucks them early, brings them home.
They merge, have no need to atone.
  Find oneness
  Find wholeness
  Find LOVE.

AURORA

Aurora rises, golden,
in Northern Cyprus
where death hangs
over bamboo and pineta
palm and bulrush
olive and orange
vine and pomegranate
strawberry and fig
swallow and kite
palaces and garbage
luxury and dereliction
Dust rises
In flower time she would be here
except she is now passed
No longer flower-time
Spring flowers spent

Aurora rises in gold
Aurora sinks in sapphire

THE WAKE

The setting sun cast a path
Beyond the dipping stern and aft.
My craft was light with one small bag.
I took no baggage else on board.
Nothing to hoard. I set my sail
though stronger hand took the tiller.
The wind carried pungency
not urgency.
Prow cleaved foaming water,
flouncing petticoat lace
into a wake which trailed
the only evidence of movement
in that oceanic vastness.
The wake woke me to the busyness of bubbling
as we ploughed our watery furrow,
foam strong and vital at its apex
dissipating into lines of nothingness,
lines which lingered only
till the bubbles disappeared
into the weight of water,
like a congregation of mourners.

THIRTY-FIRST OF DECEMBER

This is the last day.
In a way, too, it is the first day.
There has never been anything but the first day.
Thinking thus, my own thirst is assuaged.
Nothing taints the purity of the waters I drink today,
because it is the first day.
Today I am ancient, old as the hills.
I have lived so long that my edges are frayed,
like the smudged lines of a charcoal drawing.
No outline.
Formlessness comes with great age,
Through form after form, distilling and distilled
till I am stilled.
And, in this stillness of ancients,
I finally rest my case.
There is no more baggage.
Others may draw my outline,
try heaping their own stuff within its boundaries,
but to no avail.
And, as I think of the insubstantial substance of veils
through which I now pass,
my eyes fill with that same distilled water.
I weep with longing for the charcoal to be washed away
entirely.
The most delicate sable brush will finally obliterate me
and my footprints,
hush the voice to a dark night's whisper
until only a wand works wonders.

DEPARTURE

The street lamps cast shadows
Mine strong on the ground
I recognise my silhouette
That's me, a sharply defined
shadow on the pavement
The light recedes
The shadow fades
as though it never existed....

THE TIME COMETH

The old woman considered her death.
Black midnight drew near.
Her heart caressed dear loved ones
And fairies she was wont to hear –
Music now fading from her straining ear.

I COULD HAVE DIED LAUGHING

But I've decided to live laughing instead.
More fun, somehow.....

I could have kicked the bucket.
But where to?
And it's full of water.

I could have dropped off my perch.
But I'm hanging on for dear life.
Life's costly, though it's hard on the nails.

I could have passed over.
But I think I'll let that one pass.
Flying is such a business these days.

I could have left the planet.
But would I find a better one?
My satnav isn't always reliable.

I could have simply died.
But I've done that so many times already.
Nothing new, frankly.

I'm going to die.
I'm dying to go.
But this life's such a dream right now.

21 July 18

EPITAPH

HERE LIES THE FAIRY GODMOTHER

FOOD FOR CROWS

FOOD FOR WORMS

FOOD FOR THOUGHT

MAY SHE NOURISH NATURE

AS NATURE NOURISHED HER

Afterword

RE-INVENTING A WOMAN

In all her deaths she has been awaiting a life,
the life of whom she thinks she is.
In all her lives she has been awaiting a death,
the death of whom she knows she's not.
And now the one she once thought she was,
 is killed by the knife of life's affrays.

Every moment had held a choice
and as she chose, just like the rose,
she died then lived, lived then died.
And every choice had held a moment
 of living and dying, dying and living.
The summation of her moments now

brings her to the brink of... she knows not what.
Boldly, and without a blink,
she leaps into a chasm of unknowing.
Free-falling upwards, defying gravity,
the gravity of her situation.

And here she is, new-chosen, new-born.
The woman leaps. No-one else by her side.
No friend, no guide and, with nothing to hide,
all past inventions have surrendered to death.
Un-bereft, she gives birth, is the mother
of a woman re-invented.

16 Oct 18

Lynne Nesbit